VeggieTales

Big-Note Piano

And now it's time for

Silly Songs with Larry

CONTENTS

VeggieTales® is a registered trademark of Big Idea Productions, Inc.
© 2002 Big Idea Productions, Inc. All rights reserved.
Please visit the VeggieTales® website at
www.bigidea.com

ISBN 978-0-634-04107-5

HAL•LEONARD®
CORPORATION

7777 W. BLUEMOUND RD. P.O. BOX 13819 MILWAUKEE, WI 53213

For all works contained herein:
Unauthorized copying, arranging, adapting, recording or public performance is an infringement of copyright.
Infringers are liable under the law.

Visit Hal Leonard Online at
www.halleonard.com

The Dance of the Cucumber

Melody based on an Argentinean folksong
Words by MIKE NAWROCKI
Translation by LISA NAWROCKI

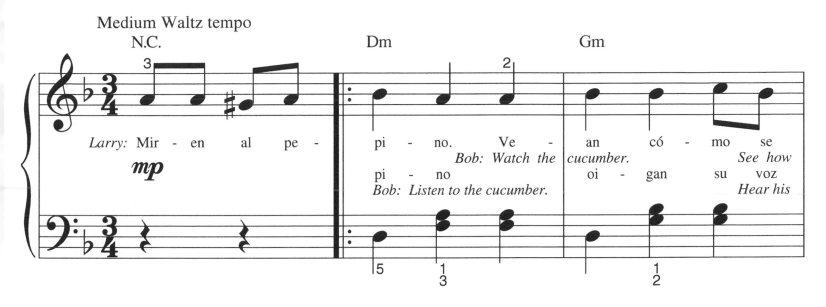

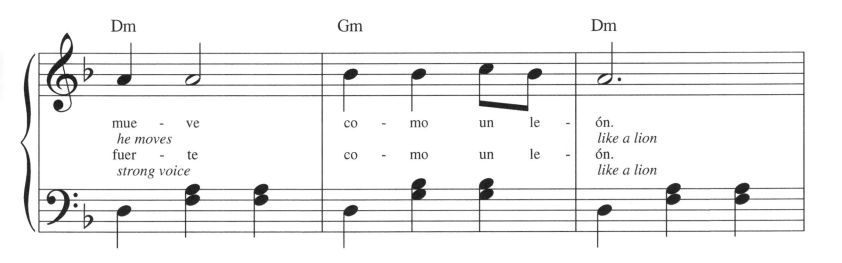

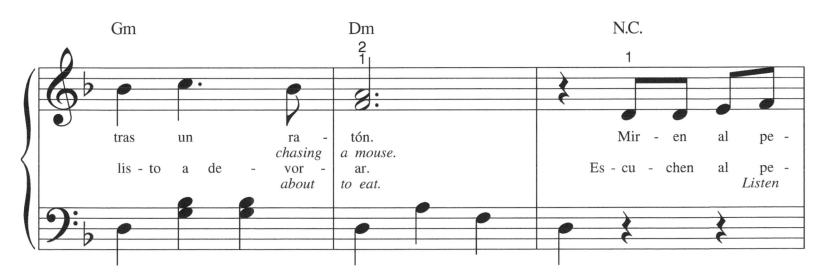

© 1995 BOB AND LARRY PUBLISHING
Admin. by EMI CHRISTIAN MUSIC PUBLISHING
All Rights Reserved   Used by Permission

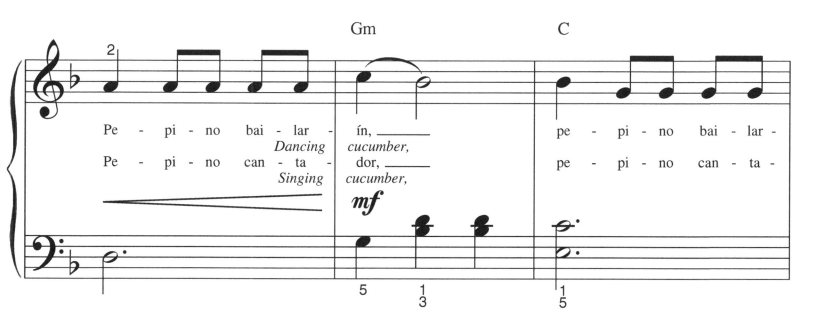

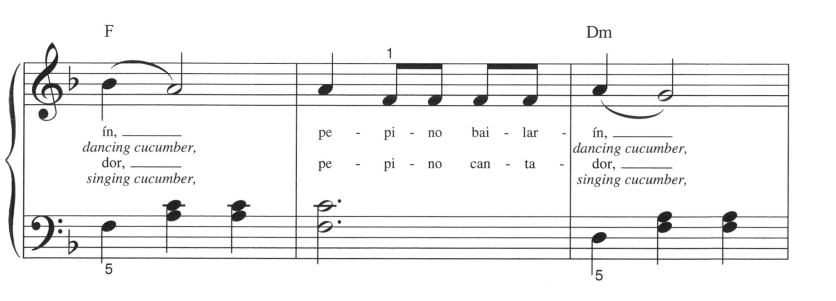

8

Endangered Love

Words by MIKE NAWROCKI
Music by MIKE NAWROCKI and KURT HEINECKE

© 2000 BOB AND LARRY PUBLISHING
Admin. by EMI CHRISTIAN MUSIC PUBLISHING
All Rights Reserved   Used by Permission

10

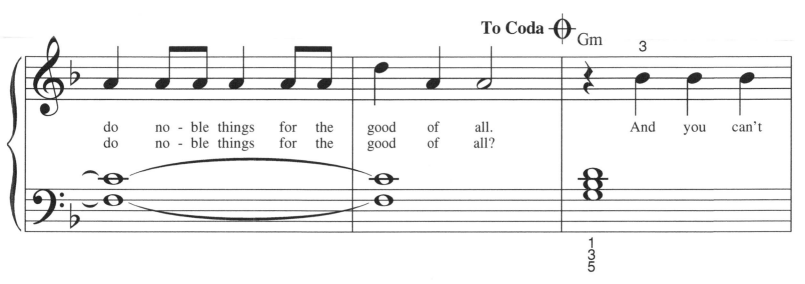

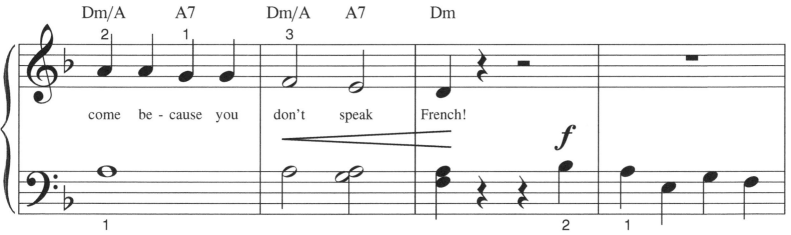

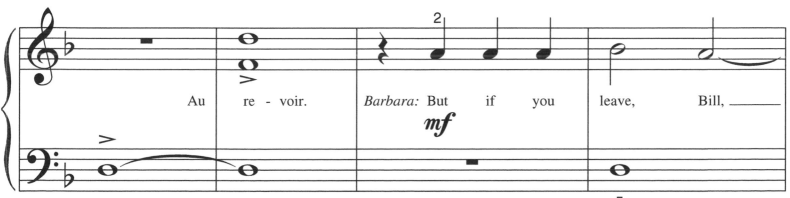

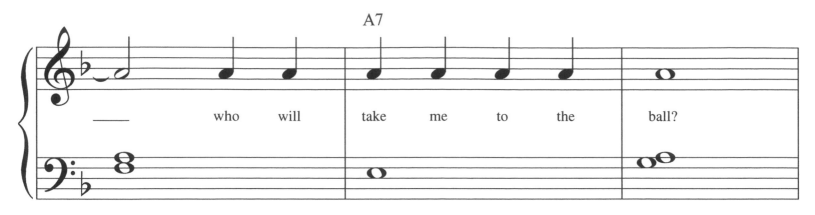

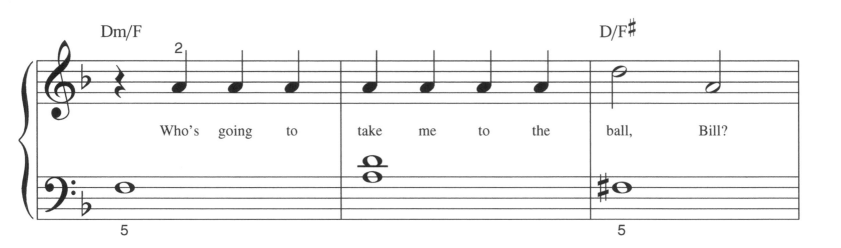

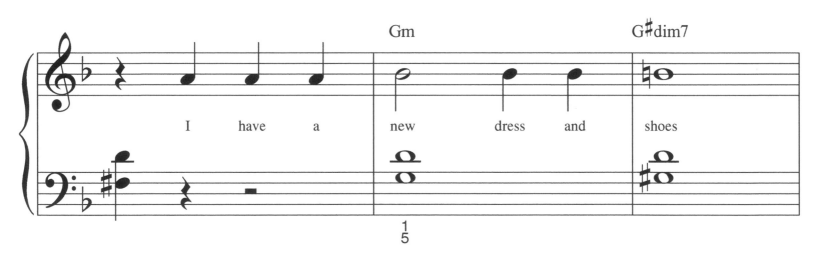

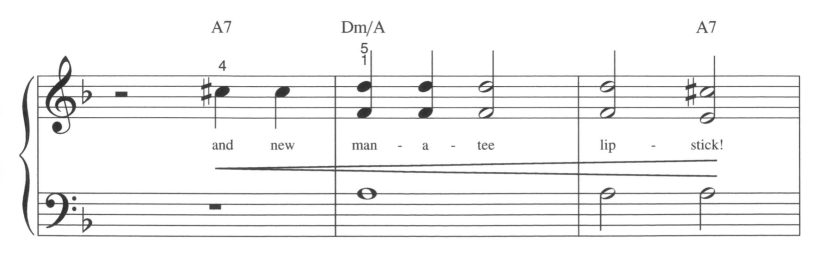

Who will take me to the ball?

Larry: Bar - b'ra Man - a - tee,

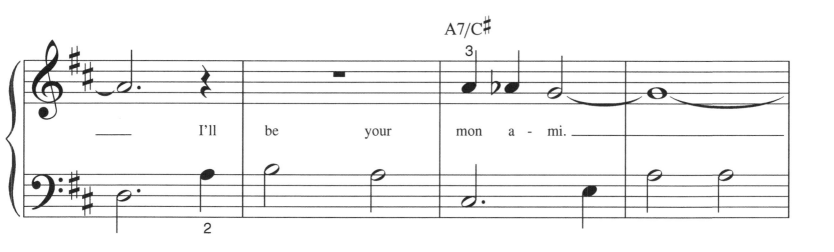

I'll be your mon a - mi.

I'll take you to the ball.

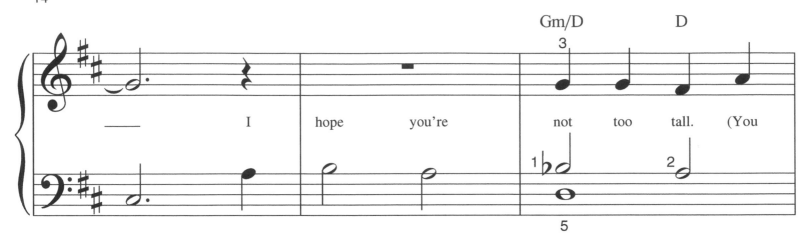

I hope you're not too tall. (You

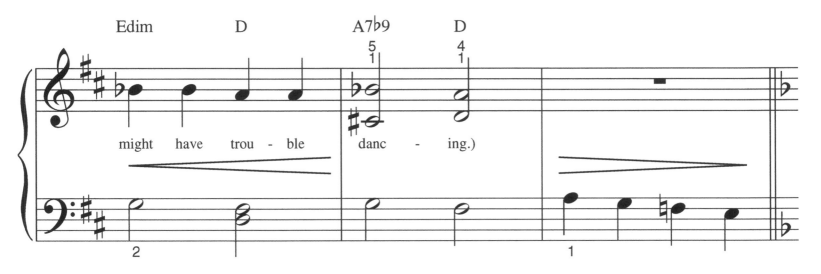

might have trou - ble danc - ing.)

Barbara: Bill, I've learned French!   *Bill: You have?*

Barbara: Mais oui!   *Je suis manatee!*

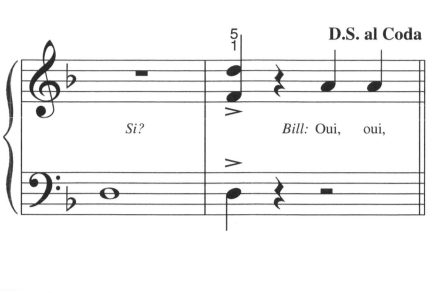

Si?   **D.S. al Coda**   **CODA**   Gm   N.C.

Bill: Oui, oui,   *Barbara:* Yes!

But first, Bill,   will you   take me to the

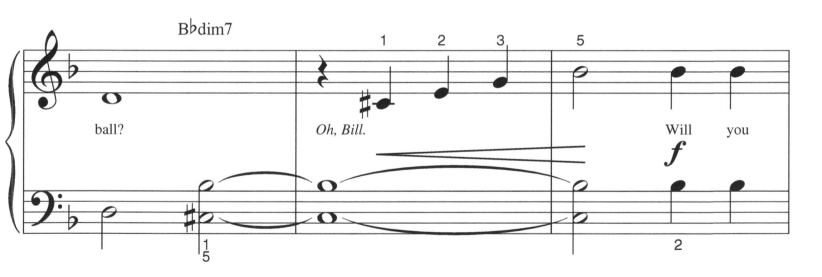

Bb dim7

ball?   *Oh, Bill.*   Will you

f

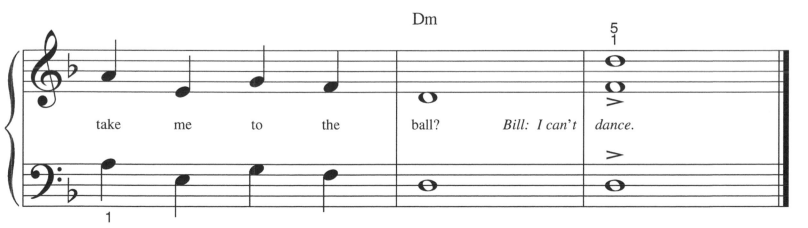

Dm

take me to the   ball?   *Bill: I can't* dance.

The Hairbrush Song

Words by MIKE NAWROCKI
Music by MIKE NAWROCKI,
LISA VISCHER and KURT HEINECKE

© 1995 BOB AND LARRY PUBLISHING
Admin. by EMI CHRISTIAN MUSIC PUBLISHING
All Rights Reserved   Used by Permission

18

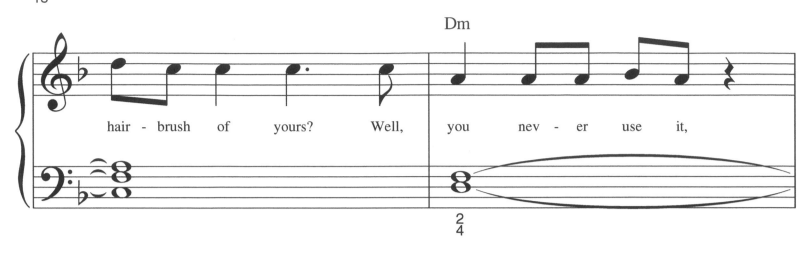

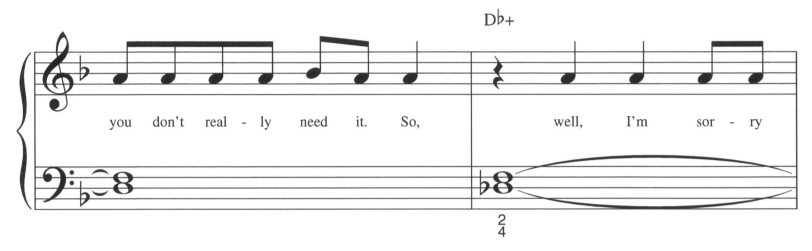

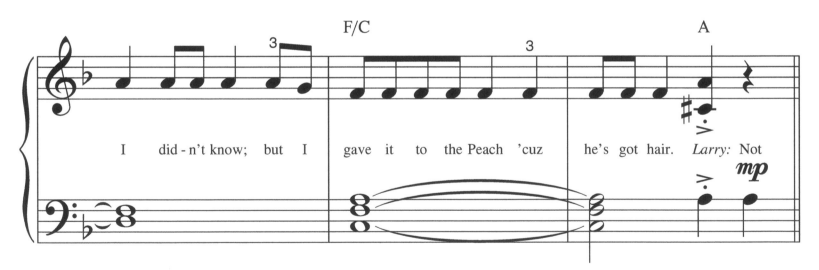

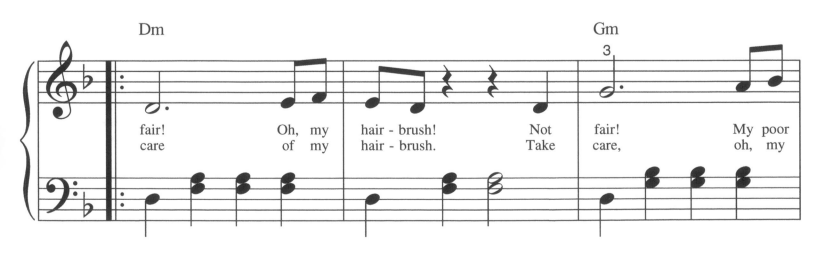

His Cheeseburger

Words by MIKE NAWROCKI
Music by MIKE NAWROCKI and KURT HEINECKE

© 1998 BOB AND LARRY PUBLISHING
Admin. by EMI CHRISTIAN MUSIC PUBLISHING
All Rights Reserved   Used by Permission

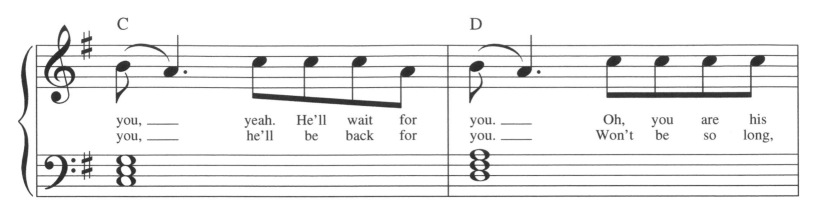

C   D

you, ____ yeah. He'll wait for you. ____ Oh, you are his
you, ____ he'll be back for you. ____ Won't be so long,

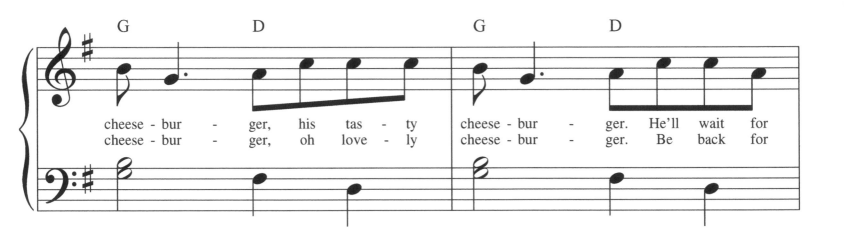

G   D   G   D

cheese - bur - ger, his tas - ty cheese - bur - ger. He'll wait for
cheese - bur - ger, oh love - ly cheese - bur - ger. Be back for

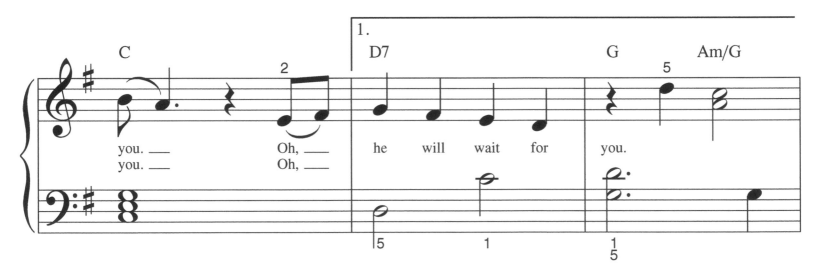

C   1.   D7   G   Am/G

you. ____ Oh, ____ he will wait for you.
you. ____ Oh, ____

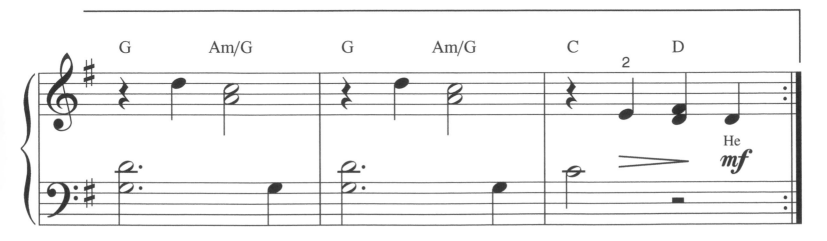

G   Am/G   G   Am/G   C   D

He
mf

Ab/Bb ... Gb/Bb

hands and knees to see if someone ac - ci - dent - ly dropped some

Bb ... C

cheese in the dirt and he would wash it off for you, wipe it off for you,

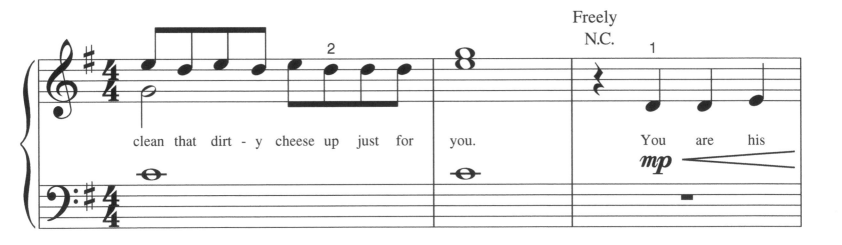

Freely
N.C.

clean that dirt - y cheese up just for you. You are his

mp

F

cheese - bur - ger.

Lost Puppies

Words and Music by
MIKE NAWROCKI

Medium Waltz tempo

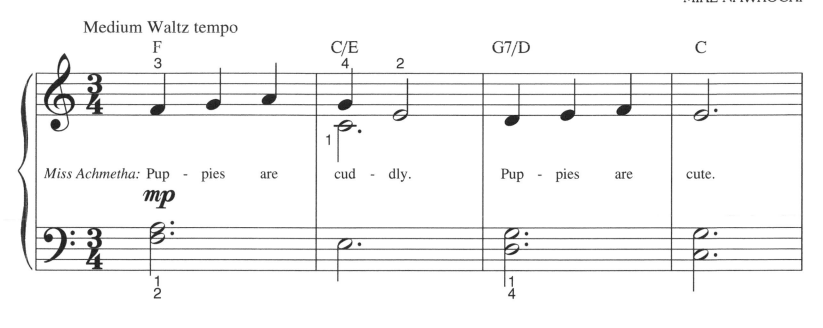

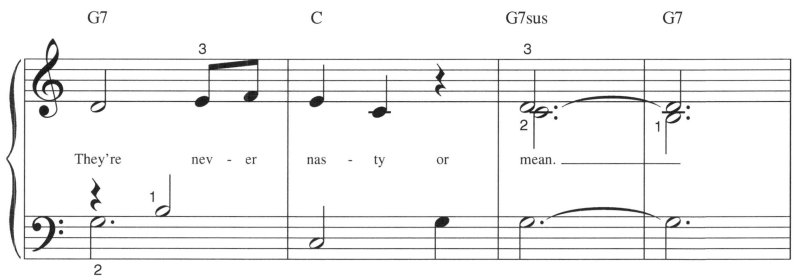

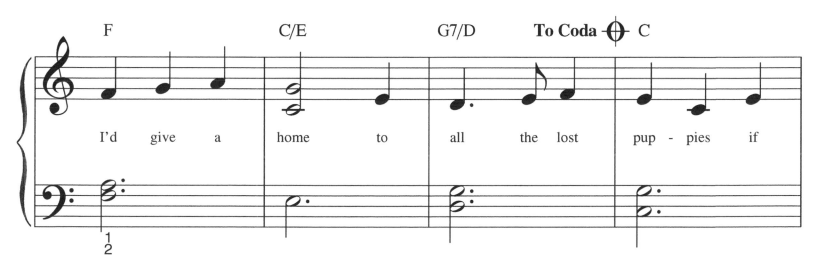

© 2000 BOB AND LARRY PUBLISHING
Admin. by EMI CHRISTIAN MUSIC PUBLISHING
All Rights Reserved   Used by Permission

Love My Lips

Words by MIKE NAWROCKI
Music by MIKE NAWROCKI and KURT HEINECKE

Moderate Country Shuffle

Larry: If my lips ev- er

left my mouth, packed a bag and head- ed south, that'd

be too bad. I'd be so sad. Archie: I

see... that'd be too bad. You'd be so sad. Larry: That'd be too

© 1996 BOB AND LARRY PUBLISHING
Admin. by EMI CHRISTIAN MUSIC PUBLISHING
All Rights Reserved   Used by Permission

29

30

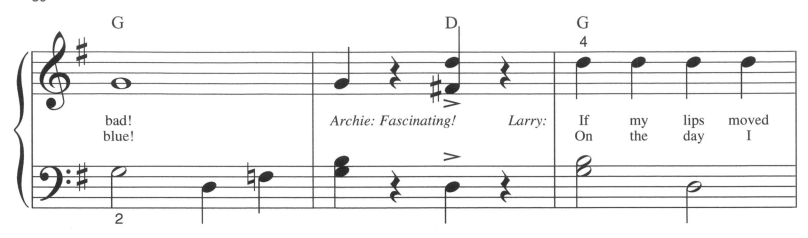

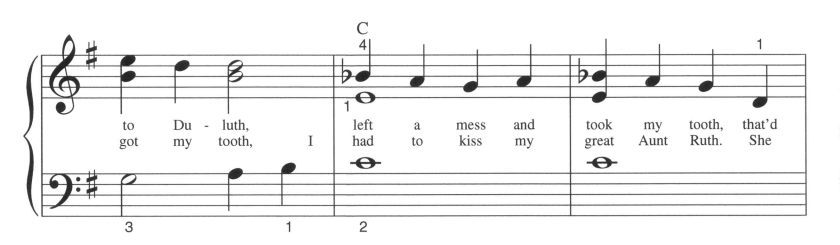

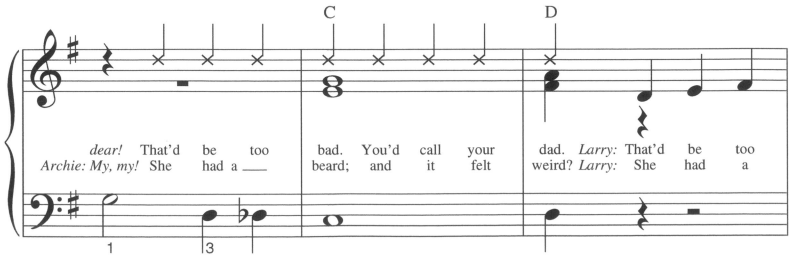

32

CODA

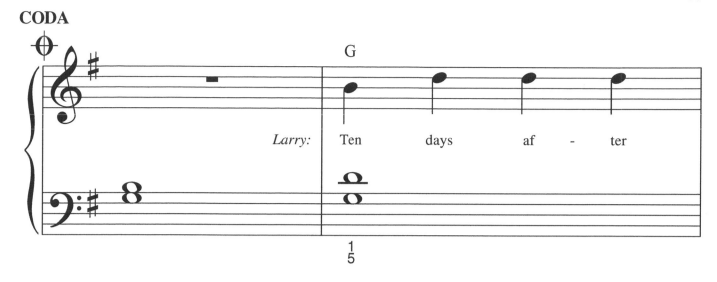

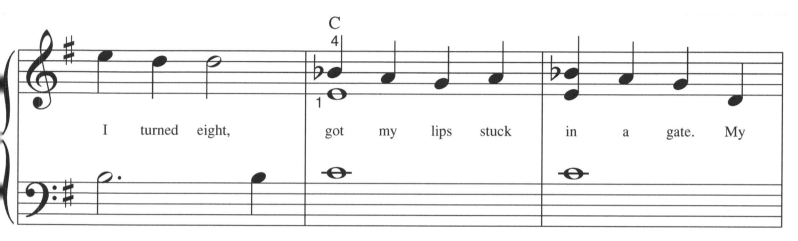

Larry: *stood there until the Fire Department came and broke the lock with a crowbar and I had to spend the next six weeks in lip rehab with this kid named Oscar who got stung by a bee right on the lip and we couldn't even talk to each other until the fifth week 'cuz both of our lips were so swollen and when we did start speaking he just spoke Polish and I only knew like three words in Polish except now I know four because Oscar taught me the word for lip, "osta."*

Archie: *Your friends all laughed… "osta"…how do you spell that?*

Larry: *I don't know.*

Archie: *So what you're saying, is that when you were young…*

34

8vb

The Pirates Who Don't Do Anything

Words by MIKE NAWROCKI
Music by MIKE NAWROCKI and KURT HEINECKE

Medium March tempo

© 1993 BOB AND LARRY PUBLISHING
Admin. by EMI CHRISTIAN MUSIC PUBLISHING
All Rights Reserved   Used by Permission

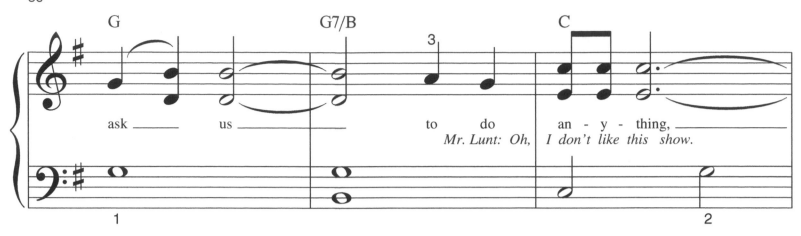

ask _____ us _____ to do an - y - thing, _____
Mr. Lunt: Oh, I don't like this show.

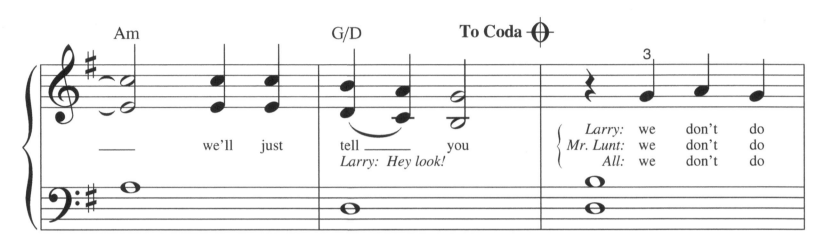

To Coda ⊕

_____ we'll just tell _____ you
Larry: Hey look!

Larry: we don't do
Mr. Lunt: we don't do
All: we don't do

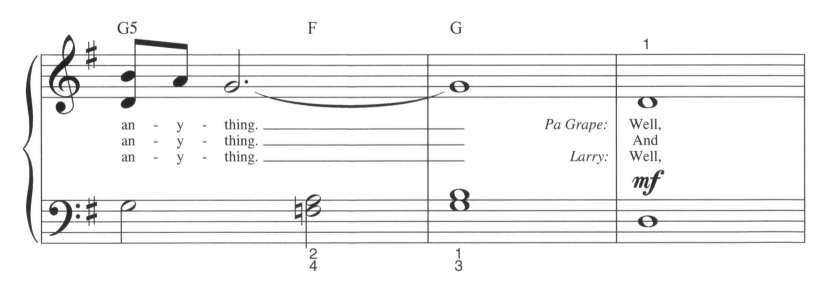

an - y - thing. _____
an - y - thing. _____
an - y - thing. _____

Pa Grape: Well,
And
Larry: Well,

mf

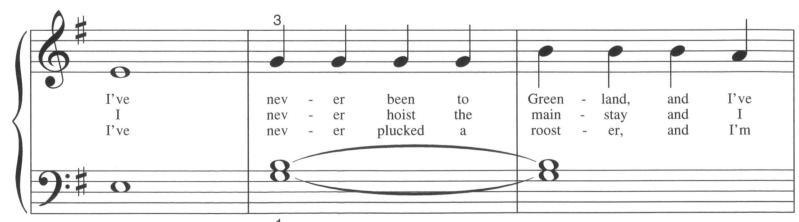

I've | nev - er been to the | Green - land, and I've
I | nev - er hoist the | main - stay and I
I've | nev - er plucked a | roost - er, and I'm

38

The Song of the Cebú

Words by MIKE NAWROCKI
Music by MIKE NAWROCKI and KURT HEINECKE

Archie: *...And what on earth is a cebú, anyway?*

Larry: *It's kind of like a cow. See?*

Archie: *Yes. Well, very good. This could be interesting. Carry on!*

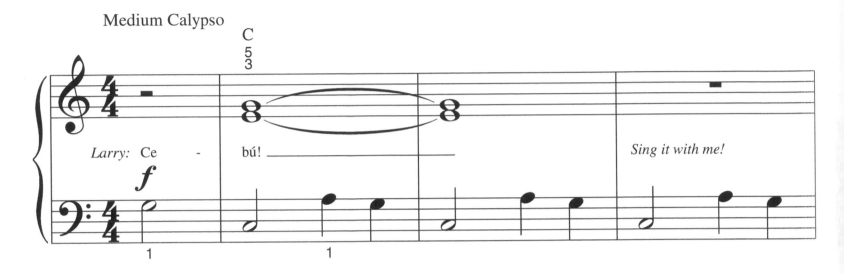

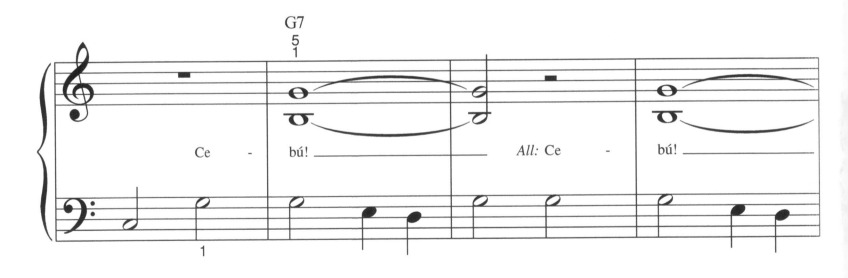

© 1993 BOB AND LARRY PUBLISHING
Admin. by EMI CHRISTIAN MUSIC PUBLISHING
All Rights Reserved   Used by Permission

C   N.C.

Larry: Boy is rid - ing with ce -

mf

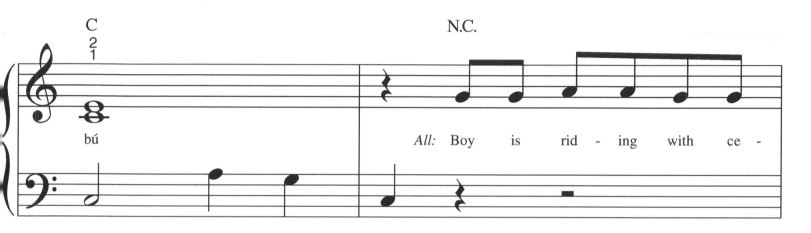

C

All: Boy is rid - ing with ce -

bú

N.C.

C

bú

N.C.

Larry: in - to town in his ca -

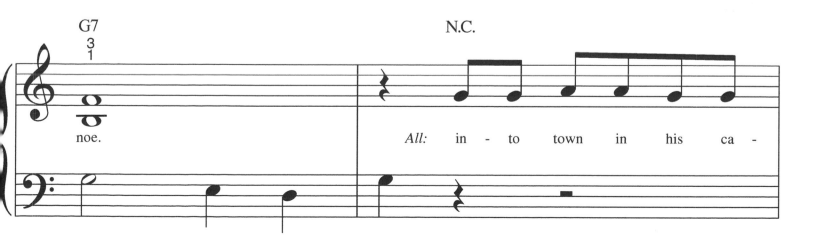

G7

noe.

N.C.

All: in - to town in his ca -

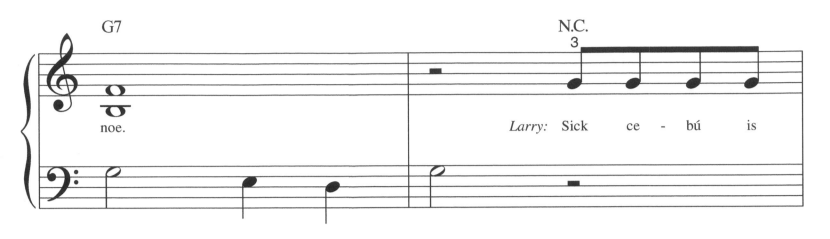

43

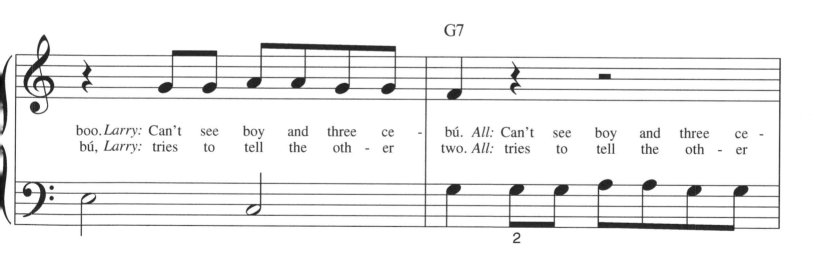

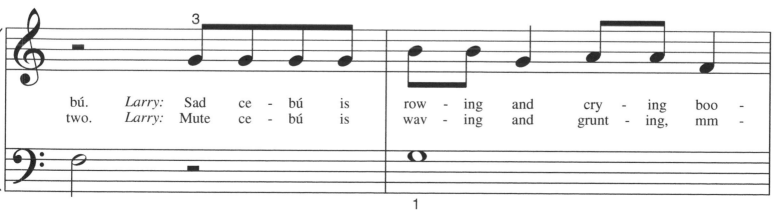

hoo moo moo, boo-hoo moo moo, boo-hoo moo moo, boo-hoo moo moo, moo,
mm mm-mm, mm-mm mm-mm, mm mm mm-mm, mm-mm mm-mm, mm

moo. *All:* Boo - hoo moo moo, boo-hoo moo moo, boo -
mm. *All:* Mm - mm mm-mm, mm-mm mm-mm, mm -

hoo moo moo, boo-hoo moo moo, boo - hoo moo moo, boo-hoo moo moo, moo,
mm mm-mm, mm-mm mm-mm, mm - mm mm-mm, mm-mm mm-mm, mm -

moo. *Larry:* Ce - bú! _____ *All:* Ce - bú! _____
mm. *f* *Larry:* Uh oh.

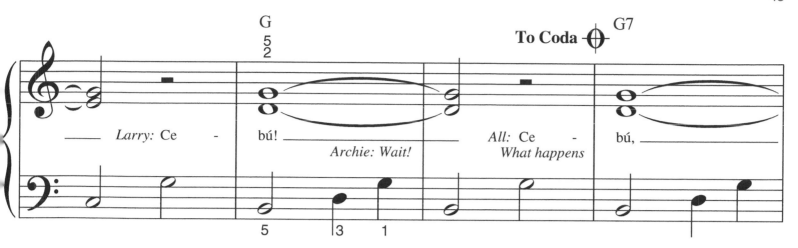

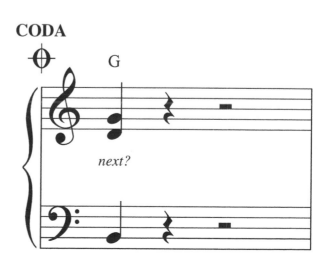

46

bye moo,   bye - bye moo,   bye -   bye moo,   bye - bye moo,   moo

C   N.C.   G7

moo.

Jimmy: I want my money back.

f

Jerry: Yeah. That'd be good.

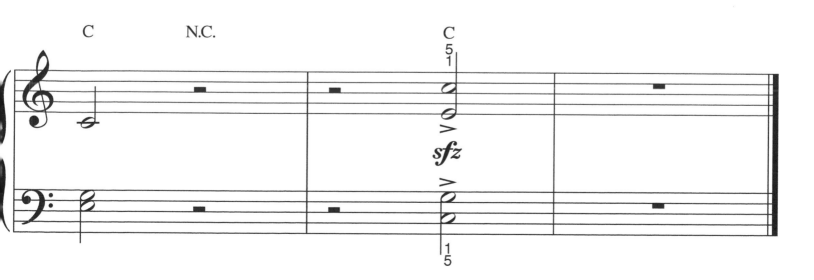

C   N.C.   C

sfz

The Water Buffalo Song

Words and Music by
PHIL VISCHER

© 1993 BOB AND LARRY PUBLISHING
Admin. by EMI CHRISTIAN MUSIC PUBLISHING
All Rights Reserved   Used by Permission

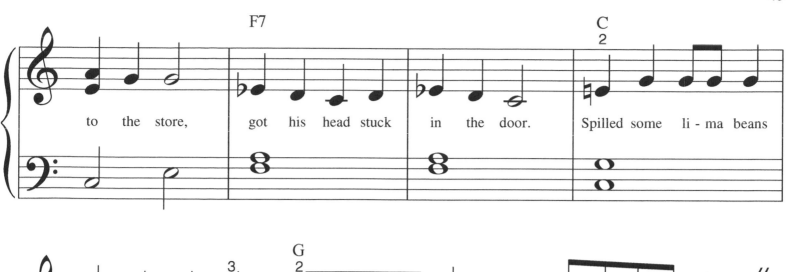

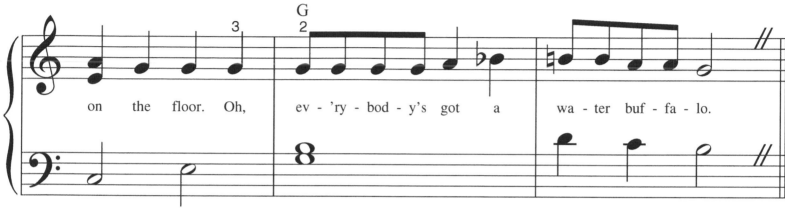

Archie: *Stop it. Stop. Stop right this instant! You can't say everybody's got a water buffalo when everyone does not have a water buffalo!*

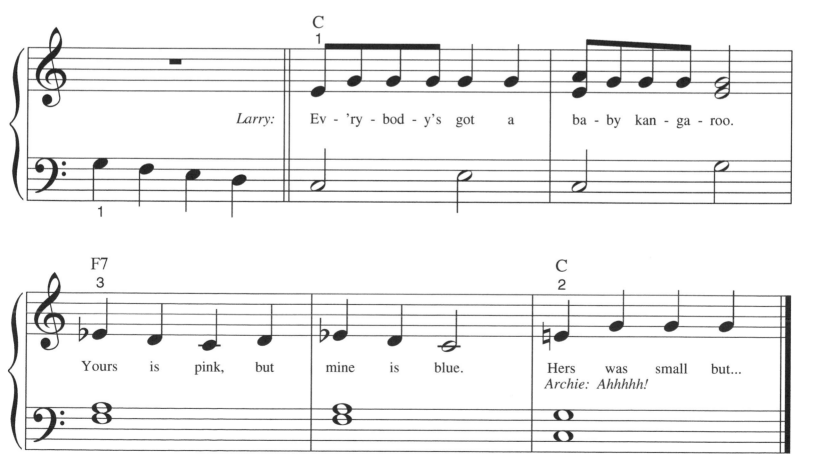

The Yodeling Veterinarian of the Alps

Words by MIKE NAWROCKI
Music by MIKE NAWROCKI and KURT HEINECKE

© 1998 BOB AND LARRY PUBLISHING
Admin. by EMI CHRISTIAN MUSIC PUBLISHING
All Rights Reserved   Used by Permission

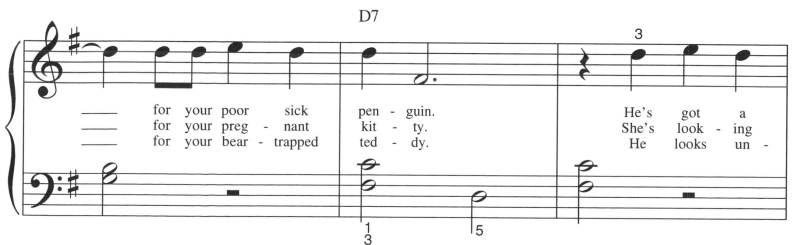

52

1.

G/D   G♯dim/D   D7

cur - i - ous ways of the   Yo - del - ing Vet - er - i - nar - i - an of the

cresc.

2.

G   N.C.

Alps.   *Larry:* "No way   Jo - sé!"

G/D   Ddim7   D7

Quartet: to the nurse of the   Yo - del - ing Vet - er - i - nar - i - an of the

cresc.

G **D.S. al Coda**

Alps!

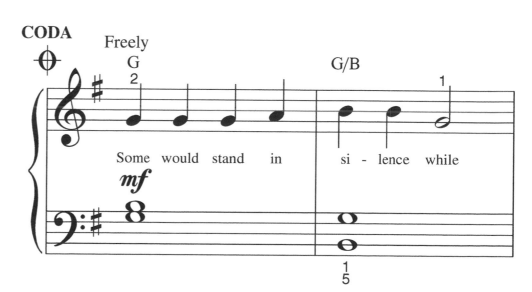

CODA
Freely

G   G/B

Some would stand in   si - lence while

mf

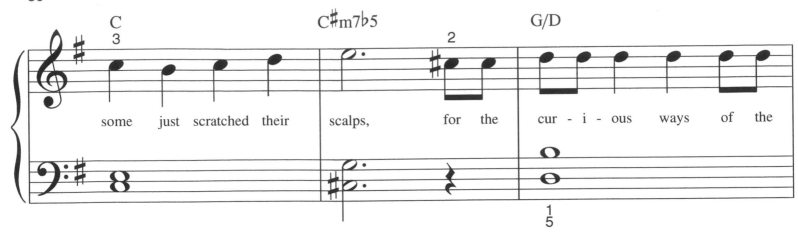

some just scratched their scalps, for the cur - i - ous ways of the

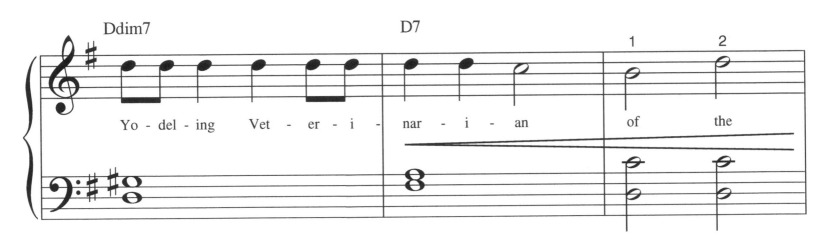

Yo - del - ing Vet - er - i - nar - i - an of the

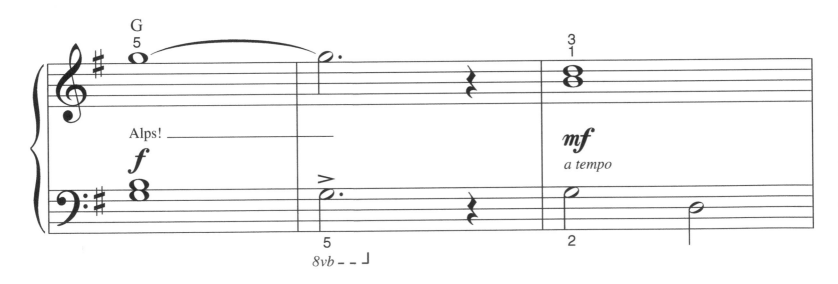

Alps! _____

a tempo

8vb